CW00540451

IMAGES OF WAR

THE BRITISH ON THE SOMME 1916

RARE PHOTOGRAPHS FROM WARTIME ARCHIVES

BOB CARRUTHERS

Pen & Sword
MILITARY

This edition published in 2017 by

Pen & Sword Military
An imprint of
Pen & Sword Books Ltd.
47 Church Street
Barnsley
South Yorkshire
S70 2AS

Copyright © Coda Publishing Ltd. 2017.
Published under licence by Pen & Sword Books Ltd.

ISBN: 9781473837812

A CIP catalogue record for this book is available from the British Library.

All rights reserved. No part of this book may be reproduced or transmitted in any form or by any means, electronic or mechanical including photocopying, recording or by any information storage and retrieval system, without permission from the Publisher in writing.

Printed and bound in England
By CPI Group (UK) Ltd., Croydon, CR0 4YY

Pen & Sword Books Ltd. incorporates the imprints of Pen & Sword Aviation, Pen & Sword Family History, Pen & Sword Maritime, Pen & Sword Military, Pen & Sword Discovery, Pen & Sword Politics, Pen & Sword Atlas, Pen & Sword Archaeology, Wharncliffe Local History, Wharncliffe True Crime, Wharncliffe Transport, Pen & Sword Select, Pen & Sword Military Classics, Leo Cooper, The Praetorian Press, Claymore Press, Remember When, Seaforth Publishing and Frontline Publishing

For a complete list of Pen & Sword titles please contact

PEN & SWORD BOOKS LIMITED
47 Church Street, Barnsley, South Yorkshire, S70 2AS, England
E-mail: enquiries@pen-and-sword.co.uk
Website: www.pen-and-sword.co.uk

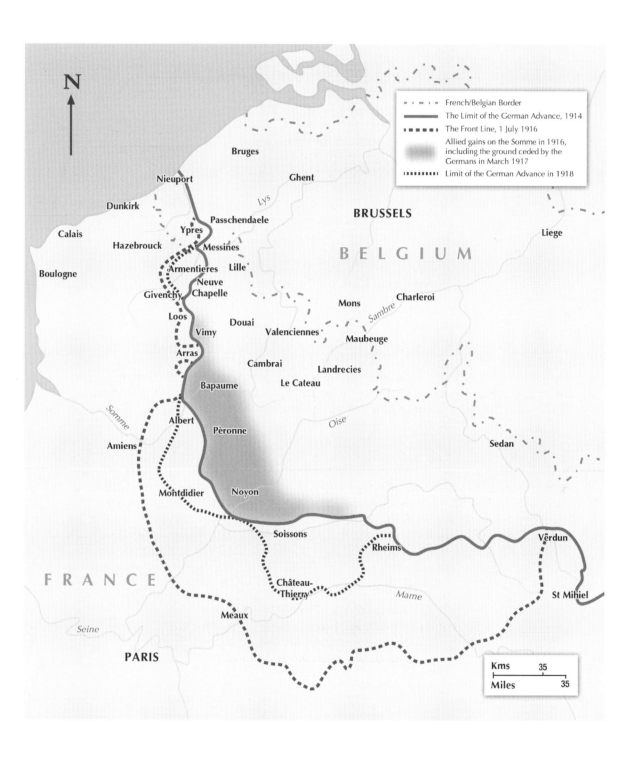

N

French/Belgian Border
The Limit of the German Advance, 1914
The Front Line, 1 July 1916
Allied gains on the Somme in 1916, including the ground ceded by the Germans in March 1917
Limit of the German Advance in 1918

Bruges

Nieuport

Ghent

Dunkirk

Calais

Passchendaele

BRUSSELS

Liege

Ypres

BELGIUM

Hazebrouck

Messines

Boulogne

Lys

Armentieres

Lille

Neuve
Chapelle

Givenchy

Mons

Charleroi

Loos

Sambre

Douai

Vimy

Valenciennes

Maubeuge

Arras

Cambrai

Landrecies

Bapaume

Le Cateau

Albert

Oise

Péronne

Sedan

Amiens

Somme

Montdidier

Noyon

Soissons

Verdun

Rheims

FRANCE

Château-
Thierry

St Mihiel

Marne

Meaux

Seine

PARIS

Kms	35
Miles	35

The British On the Somme

Ernest Brooks was the first official photographer to be appointed by the British military. He produced thousands of images between 1915 and 1918, amounting to more than a tenth of all British official photographs taken during the war with the majority of those from the Battle of the Somme. One of Brooke's earliest photographs is the famous image from July 1916, which depicts men of the 11th Cheshire Regiment resting in a captured German trench during the battle. In the famous photographic portrait of Brooks, taken by a fellow photographer, he is shown posing sternly in a trench 'somewhere on the Western Front' with his Goerz-Anschütz plate camera. That camera produced the powerful images such as the wounded British soldiers and German prisoners heading to the rear during the Somme that you will find in these pages. Ernest Brooks was soon joined by John Warwick Brooke who arrived just in time for the Battle of the Somme.

Today, many of the men who look back at us from a century ago from the official photographs captured at the Somme by Brooks and Brooke remain there. They lie in the dozens of military cemeteries which grace the landscape of Picardy. The Battle of the Somme occupies a unique place in British military history; the name resonates with the British public. Over one million men on both sides were killed or wounded in the fields which stretch northwards and just south of the Somme. Although the battle dragged on from July to mid-November it is the events of 1 July which are most remembered today.

Strategically, the Battle of the Somme was fought as part of a simultaneous series of offensives by the British, French, Italian and Russian armies, designed to place intolerable pressure on the Central Powers. With the pressure mounting at Verdun, on 16 June 1916, General Sir Douglas Haig, commander of the British Expeditionary Force, ordered that the British offensive was to be commenced in order to relieve pressure on the French at Verdun and inflict as many losses as possible on the thinly stretched German forces. The attack was to be made by five divisions of the French Sixth Army positioned either side of the Somme and thirteen British divisions of the British Fourth Army north of the Somme; the blow would fall against the German Second Army led by General Fritz von Below. After a five-day artillery bombardment, the newly-created British Fourth Army was expected to advance through the shattered German defences and capture 16 miles of the German first line from Montauban to Serre, with the cavalry to take the front forward to as far as Bapaume. The British Third Army was to mount a diversion at Gommecourt. The village of La Boisselle lay at the centre point of the British attack that was designed to push up the old Roman road leading from Albert to Bapaume.

The bombardment began on 24 June, but the attack was postponed for two days due to bad weather and finally scheduled for 1 July. The British attack, preceded by a massive artillery barrage on a hitherto unheralded scale, with 1,500 British and French guns firing over one and a half million shells into the German lines. On the British sector it was to prove a futile exercise. The bulk of the artillery was far too light to reach the deep German dug outs where the machine-gun crews awaited the moment the bombardment would lift.

The phrase 'going over the top' came into common usage during the Great war and has entered the language as a byword for ineffective fury. During the war the men on the western front in Picardy lived and fought in trenches excavated from the local chalk soil and to show oneself above the trench was suicide. For 20,000 British soldiers the order to advance was a death sentence; 40,000 more were wounded on the infamous 1 July 1916.

On the Somme front a highly effective German plan, devised in January 1915, had since been completed. The killing machine which took such a heavy toll on the British Army was based on the almost impregnable German lines of defence. The German front line had been strengthened by increasing the number of trench lines from one line to three, each set about 200 yards apart, the first trench was lightly held and occupied by sentry groups, the second line was occupied by the main front-trench garrison. The third trench held local reserves. The German trenches were traversed and had sentry-posts in recesses built into the parapet. Dugouts had been deepened to 20-30 feet they were spaced 50 yards apart and large enough for 25 men. An intermediate line of strong points (*Stutzpunktlinie*) about 1,000 yards behind the front line was also built.

Barbed wire obstacles had been enlarged from one belt which was only 5-10 yards wide to two, strong belts each 30 yards wide and about 15 yards apart. Double and triple thickness wire was used and formed into belts 3-5 feet high. The German defenders, with meticulous planning, had constructed a telephone with lines buried six feet deep for five miles behind the front line which was used to connect the front line to the artillery.

German artillery was highly effective, being organised in a series of *sperrfeuerstreifen* (or barrage sectors); each officer was expected to know the batteries covering his section of the front line and the batteries were constantly ready to engage even the most fleeting of targets. Despite their strengths the German defences however had two inherent weaknesses which the rebuilding had not remedied. The German front trenches were invariably located on a forward slope, where they were clearly out-lined by the white chalk spoil from the subsoil from which the trenches were excavated and as a result they were visible to all. The defending forces were also concentrated towards the front trench.

In addition to the massive artillery barrage, other preparations were made including exploding two colossal mines under the German trenches on either side of the village of La Boisselle and another near Beaumont-Hamel. Despite all of the preparations the opening day of the battle was a disaster. On the opening day of the battle the British Army suffered a crushing defeat suffering 60,000 casualties in a single day 20,000 of whom were killed.

The men fighting to the north of La Boisselle were photographed by Ernest Brooks and others like him. They had advanced in confident expectation that the huge seven day artillery bombardment by 1,500 guns of all calibres would have destroyed the German defences. They were proved wrong. It is sobering to consider the fact that many of the men who look into the camera for Brooks now lie in one of the hundreds of cemeteries which mark the landscape.

South of La Boisselle, the Gordons and the Devons enjoyed a small measure of success on their sector of the front. The village of Mametz was captured after a well executed assault. One other that achieved a small measure of success were the valiant men of the 36th Ulster Division, who actually took the German frontline trenches. They and the twenty other British Divisions who took part in the action on 1 July are commemorated by dozens of events and ceremonies that take place every year on the battlefield, which range from informal local events to very sombre formal affairs.

Towards the end of the day the only signs which even hinted at success were the steady strickle of German prisoners who were brought in from the Fricourt–Mametz sector and assembled near the village of Carnoy. Most of these were the men from a single regiment, the 109th Reserve Infantry Regiment from Baden, and a few were from the 23rd Infantry Regiment, which recruited mainly in Silesia.

The Battle of the Somme raged on for 141 days in total without a major strategic breakthrough or even reaching those objectives which had been designated for capture on the first day. By the end of the battle the Anglo-French armies had failed to capture Péronne and were still 3 miles from Bapaume, an objective that was supposed to have been captured by the cavalry on the first day. The slim gains that were won came at a cost of 419,654 British casualties against an estimated 200,000 German casualties who were lost on the British sector. At the end of the five month long offensive on 22 November 1916, the British and French forces had penetrated just six miles into German-occupied territory, on a front which was 16 miles long.

Until the 1930s the dominant view of the battle was that the Somme was a hard-fought victory against a brave, experienced and well-led opponent. However, during the 1960s the view changed and the popular conception took hold that the battle was a futile slaughter planned by incompetents. The British generals Haig and Rawlinson have been characterised as stubborn, pig headed, obstinate and slow to learn. The very name of the battle has become a byword for waste, and futility. The resulting debate on the topic has lasted for one hundred years. In recent years a more nuanced version of the original orthodoxy has arisen, which does not seek to minimize the human cost of the battle, but sets it in the context of industrial warfare in which the only long term option was to defeat comparable opponents through a war of exhaustion.

Regardless of the view we hold, we can be thankful that photographers Ernest Brooks and John Warwick Brooke were on hand to produce a primary record these historic events for posterity.

Two weeks after the start of the massive bombardment, the Somme battlefield had become a wasteland, with many hundreds of unburied bodies strewn across it. Undaunted by their limited success, the British and French continued with the offensive.

Summer 1916 – Sir Douglas Haig with General Joffre, the chief of the French General Staff and commander-in-chief in the field. Regardless of heavy losses, difficult operational conditions for the men at the front and disappointing results, the two commanders pressed on with their offensive.

28 June 1916 – The 4th Battalion, the Worcestershire Regiment (29th Division), resting on their way to the trenches, at Louvencourt. Wire cutters can be seen attached to their rifles.

A battalion of the London Scottish marching to the trenches at the northernmost part of the Somme battlefield.

June 1916 – British 8-inch Howitzers were essential to the bombardments due to their capacity to send shells over 10,000 yards. By June 1916, there were 64 in use.

June 1916 – Soldiers prepare a British 15-inch Howitzer for firing. With the ability to throw high explosive shells weighing more than half a tonne nearly 11,000 yards, these were deadly machines.

An 8-inch howitzer is towed in to position by a Holt track laying tractor. With their practical tracks and 75 horsepower petrol engine, the Holts were to provide inspiration for the tanks, which made their first appearance on the battlefields on 15 September, during the Somme.

Various types of warning bells and rattles were used during the war; in particular these were sounded in the event of a gas attack. This gas sentry is wearing an early form of gas hood impregnated with hyposulphate of soda and phenate to protect the wearer.

8-inch Howitzer shells await transportation to battery positions. Their boxed fuses lie in front of them. Numerous ammunition dumps like this were established in the rear areas, sited as close as practicable to a railway line.

The barrage which preceded the Battle of the Somme began on 24 June. In the week that followed 1,732,873 shells were fired by British guns along the 14 miles of front.

A British 9.2-inch gun, mounted on a specially designed railway wagon, fires on German positions during the preliminary bombardment.

A contemporary illustration of a heavy British howitzer on a rail emplacement shelling the German positions in the hope of laying the foundations for the success of the infantry attack to follow.

During the initial bombardment the British fired over 1.7 million rounds. The sheer scale of the shelling is indicated by this dump of 18-pounder shell cases, located on the battlefield.

King George V came to France to visit his troops in the field at Rawlinson's headquarters at Querrieu. At the foot of the steps (from left to right), Sir Henry Rawlinson, Sir Douglas Haig, and King George.

A British camp on the eve of the great offensive. The dusty roads were alive with movement and, in the foreground, the men can be seen collecting their equipment for the coming ordeal.

30 June 1916 – Two infantry men converse on the evening before the Somme Offensive. The relaxed atmosphere in this picture is a sharp contrast to what was coming the following morning; I July 1916, would go down as one of the worst days in British military history.

Men of the Lancashire Fusiliers being addressed by their divisional commander, Major General Beauvoir de Lisle, on the eve of the great battle.

The British howitzers continue to pound the German trenches in the build up to the 'Big Push'. In addition to a shortage of such guns, much of the ammunition failed to detonate.

Unlike the boggy clay of the Ypres Salient, the Somme had a chalk subsoil that allowed for easier tunnelling. Here, men of a Royal Engineers tunnelling company work in a mine chamber. The officer on the left has a stethoscope-type arrangement, used to listen for working by German miners.

July 1916 – The scene in a communication trench in the build up to the opening phase of the offensive, which was later known as the Battle of Albert.

Commonly believed to be a company of the 1st Public Schools Battalion (16th Battalion, the Middlesex Regiment) at the White City, near Beaumont-Hamel prior to the Battle of the Somme.

1 July 1916 – In preparation for the assault on Beaumont, on the morning of the Somme Offensive's opening day, the 1st Battalion Lancashire Fusiliers fix bayonets.

1 July 1916 – After seven days of bombardment, the Battle of Albert began with the firing of the Hawthorn Mine near Beaumont-Hamel. The explosion was filmed by Geoffrey Malins and features prominently in the famous Somme documentary.

1 July 1916 – A battalion of the 103rd (Tyneside Irish) Brigade advances shortly after zero hour during the British attack on La Boisselle.

Minutes later, men desperately seek some cover from German machine-gun fire and shells. In the middle distance two men bravely seek to recover the wounded to safety.

1 July 1916 – British troops launching an attack on the German lines. The trenches are clearly indicated by the brilliant white from excavated chalk, never far from the surface on the Somme battlefield. The figures of the advancing men can be seen against the white of the trenches.

During the early stages of the battle a trench in the support lines is used for a well-earned rest by a ration party of the Royal Irish Rifles.

Men of the 1st Battalion Lancashire Fusiliers fix bayonets in readiness for an attack on the Somme.

During the afternoon of the first day of the battle, the Seaforth Highlanders assemble for roll call north of Beaumont-Hamel.

Captured German trenches near La Boisselle show two of the major problems faced by the British: complex belts of barbed wire defences and deep dugout shelters. The lack of sufficient heavy artillery left many of the defenders' dugouts undamaged; whilst the Germans were diligent in replacing barbed wire defences that got damaged during the lengthy bombardment prior to the attack.

The film of the *Battle of the Somme* made clear to the people at home, through images such as this of a dead soldier of the 7th Division, the human cost of war and the reality of the intensive fighting on the Somme in the summer and autumn of 1916.

As the war progressed, artillery became more and more significant. The new technology available to the gunner of both sides, such as instantaneous fuses, made their weapons ever more effective, and important in operations.

To assist their assault, the 18th Division made use of flame projectors. In this case they were not mobile, and so the effect was one of 'shock and awe'; men confronted by a blast from a weapon such as this would have had to have had very strong nerves.

It is a generalization to say that the initial bombardment on the Somme failed to cut the German wire. In many cases it did, but the Germans were adept at taking advantage of darkness to repair it. At the opening of the Somme the British did not have either an appropriate shell or fuze for efficient wire cutting.

A badly wounded man is brought back to an aid post via a communication trench during the fighting on 1 July.

I July 1916 – British soldiers cautiously working their way across the shell-swept plains of Picardy. This photograph illustrates how open and exposed much of the Somme battlefield was; the two soldiers above seek to make the best of whatever cover is available.

1 July 1916 – Officers of the Royal Engineers in a communication trench on the Somme standing in front of a HQ dugout.

One of the iconic stills from the Somme film showing a badly wounded man being brought to a communication trench, probably to an advanced dressing station: similar to the photograph on page 35, it is known that the wounded man in this case died very soon afterwards.

In this still from the Somme film, taken towards the southern end of the British attack line, at Minden Post, members of the 1st Royal Welsh Fusiliers (22 Brigade, 7th Division) look curiously at a group of German prisoners. In contrast to the almost total failure of the attack in the north, there was much more success to the south and in the French sector.

Although the Royal Army Medical Corps had quite a sophisticated system to manage casualties, the sheer number of them on 1 July overwhelmed the system. In an area known as the White City, near Beaumont-Hamel, the photograph shows the busy activity around a dressing station.

Wounded British soldiers seen alongside German prisoners.

This image of an officer leading his raiding party under heavy shell fire has become one of the most enduring images from the Battle of the Somme.

A very happy looking group of gunners load the new model 6-inch howitzer that fired a hundred pound shell just under 9 kilometres. However, there were too few heavy guns available to the British on 1 July.

A dump for shell cases and boxes illustrates the sheer volume of artillery fire that characterized the battles of the Great War as both sides produced artillery pieces and shells in vast quantities.

A British ammunition convoy on a road near Albert; getting ammunition forward to the guns was a major logistics challenge.

1 July 1916 – An early batch of German prisoners is escorted into captivity under the gaze of curious British onlookers.

The Medical Officer of the 12th East Yorkshires carries out a foot inspection in a support trench. Prolonged exposure of the feet to the damp, unsanitary, and cold conditions of life in the trenches could lead to 'trench foot', which, if left untreated, in bad cases could lead to gangrene and amputation.

British troops make use of a deepened ditch alongside a sunken road that provides them with relatively secure cover. Note packs and rifles stacked on the road side of the 'trench'.

1 July 1916 — Near Beaumont-Hamel, two injured soldiers, one assisting the other, crawl to safety. They have discarded their rifles and much of their equipment, but have hung on to their helmets and haversacks containing their gas masks. Note the nature of the barbed wire entanglements.

In relative security in a trench away from the immediate fighting zone, a roll call is being taken; note that the men have removed their kit but retained their helmets. The first day alone cost almost 60,000 casualties – killed, wounded and missing – of whom 19,240 were fatalities.

July 1916 – A German trench, fairly recently captured by the British between Ovillers and the Bapaume road. Note that the position has been 'reversed', so that the back of the trench is now the front of it. A basic fire-step has been provided for the sentry, a member of A Company, 11th Battalion the Cheshire Regiment. His exhausted comrades grab any space to rest – the old fire-step, the floor of the trench or just leaning against the trench wall. The photograph is rich in detail of trench construction and soldiers' equipment.

A horse-drawn waggon and a lorry struggle through the thick mud and potholes – some of them possibly caused by shells – on the Aveluy–Albert road later in the battle.

Despite spectacular losses, the Somme offensive was not without initial gains. The French in particular made excellent progress on the first day. This photograph was taken near Fricourt, towards the south of the British front, which fell on 2 July.

July 1916 – A gun crew stands in their camouflaged emplacement near Carnoy (at the south of the British Somme front) with their 8-inch Mk V howitzer. It fired a 200 pound shell with a range of 9,600 metres. Howitzers provided plunging fire, best equipped for dealing with deeper dugouts and shelters.

The scale of the national effort involved in the war is again illustrated in this photograph. Men of the Army Ordnance Corps (it became 'Royal' in 1918) play cards on a dump of inert 'toffee apple' mortar ammunition at Acheux, several kilometres behind Beaumont-Hamel.

Prisoners wait in a trench as others, with their escorts, cross it by the use of a trench bridge. Notice that none of the Germans have a steel helmet: they only became general issue well into the battle and in the first weeks they were handed over as 'trench stores'. The great bulk of the early production of the first *stahlhelm* went to the Verdun front.

The Germans had held the same positions, with very little exception, on the Somme front for almost two years and had not been slow to develop defensive systems, both physical and in reaction planning. They dug numerous dugouts, but the one illustrated, in Bernafay Wood and captured by the 9th (Scottish) Division on 3 July, is a particularly large and fine specimen.

A group of British soldiers photographed near La Boisselle on 3 July. German prisoners are carrying a wounded man on a stretcher. Note the soldier carrying a water can at the rear of the column. The weather was changeable in the early days of the offensive; ground sheets were designed to be adaptable for use as a rain cape.

On 7 July, Mametz Wood was attacked by men of the 38th (Welsh) and 17th (Northern) divisions. After several days of notoriously fierce fighting, the wood was finally cleared of Germans on 12 July. In the distance the remains of the wood may be seen. In the foreground are piles of soldiers' kit – note the covers for the magazines, breech, bolt and trigger on some of the rifles.

July 1916 – British troops, probably medical orderlies, stand at the entrance of a German dugout in Dantzig Alley, part of the German defence, captured by the British on 1 July on the right of the line.

July 1916 – Men of the Royal Warwickshire Regiment resting near Jacob's Ladder, Beaumont-Hamel.

11 July 1916 – The indignity of death in war is eloquently shown here – German dead in a captured trench.

Wounded British soldiers who have been treated at a dressing station wait to be transported to a casualty clearing station for further treatment. If more attention was required they would be sent on to a base hospital or back to the UK.

Soldiers – some of whom are stretcher bearers – near Mametz Wood begin the arduous task of digging-in, which might in due course become part of a trench system. Note the folded stretchers in the foreground.

July 1916 – British troops digging basic shelters near Mametz Wood: one thinks that he has done enough to allow him to grab some sleep.

July 1916 – Barbed wire at Beaumont-Hamel. The impenetrable nature of this type of defence is clear from this photograph.

A common sight on any battlefield of the Great War – damaged transport (in this case a limber) pushed off to the side of a road. Note the soldier on the right of the photograph and the weight and variety of kit that he is carrying.

Taken at the beginning of the Battle of Bazentin Ridge (14–17 July), men at an Advanced (or Main) Dressing Station take advantage of the offerings of a refreshment hut. Note the highland soldier – the kilt did provide some challenges in the circumstances of the fighting in the war.

July 1916 – A brigadier general and his two staff officers examine a map in the tangled undergrowth of Mametz Wood. Despite the number of men in his command – somewhere around 4,500 – the staff of brigade headquarters was surprisingly – to modern minds – small.

The supply of water for men and animals was a problem on any battlefield. The Somme provided a bigger problem than most because of the few rivers and its geology. An Australian and a British soldier are filling water cans at a waterpoint that has been established just off the Albert–Bapaume road, near Pozières.

15 July 1916 – 18th King George's Own Lancers near Fricourt, on the Somme.

Off a road between Fricourt and Mametz Wood, a group of soldiers wearing fighting order are shown in a relaxed mood. Note the fleet of motor ambulances behind them.

High explosive shells bursting beyond the shattered remnants of Mametz Wood.

Men and machines of the Machine Gun Corps (Motors). Being motorised meant that the guns could be moved around relatively easily and quickly as circumstances dictated. They came under the corps commander. Nearly all the men on the bikes are wearing some form of German headgear.

Vickers machine-gun crew wearing PH-type anti-gas helmets near Ovillers, during the Battle of the Somme. The gunner is wearing a padded waistcoat, enabling him to carry a spare machine-gun barrel; his No. 2 is feeding the belt into the gun, to prevent blockages.

July 1916 – A British soldier brings his Lewis gun in to action near Ovillers. The Lewis gun has the advantage of being lighter than the Vickers, which it complemented rather than replaced.

July 1916 – Men of the 29th Division load ammunition on to General Service wagons at Acheux, a few kilometres behind the northern part of the Somme front. Because of the massive expansion of munitions production in a very short space of time, there was a very high proportion of shells that failed to detonate.

July 1916 – A heliograph from a pile of signalling equipment is adapted as a mirror by a resourceful soldier of the 1st Australian Division, who is taking advantage of a period out of the line to have a shave. Note that he has an identification disc hanging from a primitive belt.

A piper accompanies his comrades of the 9th (Scottish) Division as they head out of the fighting of Delville Wood on 19 July. The fighting in the wood was very fierce (it was not finally captured for another seven weeks) and is particularly associated with the South African Brigade, part of the Division since late April 1916.

An interesting photograph of British and French soldiers in July 1916, taken at the southern end of the British line and the northern part of the French one. The massive effort of the French army in the Battle of the Somme is often neglected: it suffered some 200,000 casualties during its course.

19 July 1916 – Walking wounded, including a German, make their way to a dressing station near Bernafay Wood following fighting on Bazentin Ridge.

A transport column passes the shattered remnants of Delville Wood. Every regular regiment of the British Army bar one had a battalion that was engaged in the fighting in or close to it during the summer of 1916. South Africa chose this wood as the site of its memorial in Europe.

July 1916 – Men of the 8th Black Watch relax after their involvement in the early fighting for Longueval and Delville Wood.

29 July 1916 – Some men of the 89th Infantry Brigade attend a religious service in a valley near Carnoy before going into the line. The proximity of death and the hideous sites on the battlefield often confirmed men's faith or led to them abandoning it.

This and the photograph on the following page was taken by a British official photographer in late July/early August near Thiepval Wood. Men from the Border Regiment resting in funk (or fox) holes, shelters scraped out of the trench wall. Note one of the men's kit neatly laid out.

One man stands guard whilst his exhausted comrades of the Border Regiment take the opportunity to grab some sleep. Ernest Brooks, who took these photographs, was the first official photographer appointed (March) by the British on the Western Front. The Australians and Canadians were quicker off the mark with their appointments to this task.

August 1916 – Near Bouzincourt, men of the Wiltshire Regiment return from the front with German caps, *pickelhaube* and a prisoner.

Soldiers enjoy a moment of lightheartedness as they joke about for the camera with a hansom cab that has seen better days, found in Bazentin le Grand.

7 August 1916 – Infantry from the Wiltshire Regiment pushing through the wire near Thiepval.

Taken in August 1916, this photograph shows a soldier at the entrance to a captured concrete shelter, a relative rarity on this front and at this stage of the war. Note the coverings for the working parts and the muzzles of the rifles.

8-inch howitzers of 39th Siege Battery, Royal Garrison Artillery, in action in the valley between Fricourt and Mametz in August 1916. Increased munitions production meant that the British had considerably more guns available of this type and calibre by the end of the Somme.

Men of the Australian 9.2-inch howitzer battery in action near Fricourt. The gun fired a 130kg shell to a maximum range of some 9,000 metres. Note the railway track on the left of the picture; the men in the left foreground are preparing the shells.

A well organised dressing station near Fricourt stands in an area made a desolate wasteland by the weapons and ravages of a major offensive.

The largely forgotten casualties of the Great War were the animals who served in it. Over eight million horses died during the course of the conflict. The logistics of keeping the horses healthy was a huge undertaking, every division having its own veterinary unit, whilst immense amounts of forage were required to feed the animals, most of which was shipped over from England.

Ammunition limbers of 35th (Heavy) Battery, Royal Field Artillery, pass by the pathetic remnants of Delville Wood.

September 1916 – A 60-pounder, 5-inch heavy field gun being pulled by draught horses. Despite the strength of these beasts, this was the largest gun that horses could practically manage to move.

Soldiers in support positions wait for their moment to take part in an attack near Ginchy. Note the Lewis gun in the foreground and the boxes of munitions – likely grenades and ammunition – to the right rear.

By 9 September, the Battle of Ginchy, the tactically crucial village of Guillemont had finally fallen to the British (on 3 September). The photograph shows yet another utterly destroyed wood (Trônes) and makeshift trenches between it and Guillemont.

With shells bursting on the horizon, infantry supporting the attack on Ginchy on 9 September make their way forward from trenches in the foreground.

September 1916 – Yet another shattered village: the main street of Flers. Once secure behind the German second line, the village was captured at the opening of the third phase of the Somme, the Battle of Flers–Courcelette, on 15 September, an attack assisted by the first use of tanks.

The use of smokescreens was just one of the methods used to assist in an attack. By the end of the war, the French had introduced a very efficient smoke generation system that was both quick and covered a significant area.

Men of the 16th (Irish) Division are transported to the rear after their involvement in the successful attacks at Guillemont and Ginchy.

A major problem for both sides after a successful attack lay in the shattered landscapes, criss-crossed with trenches and pitted by shell holes. This made it very difficult to move any form of wheeled transport forward, as is graphically illustrated by this photograph.

In an area where access to water was always a problem, soldiers make use of a water filled crater to carry out their ablutions. It would be well not to look too closely into the water, however; bodies – human and horses – were often concealed in their depths.

September 1916 – A gun crew operates an 8-inch howitzer in Aveluy Wood. These guns had a maximum rate of fire of two rounds a minute. Note, on the left of the gun, a row of shells ready to be fired. These would need to be cleaned before loading – dirty shells would damage the rifling of the barrel and hence the accuracy of the gun.

September 1916 – Soldiers leaning on a pile of 18-pounder shells near Bécourt Wood. Although the British had an adequate number of this type of gun, the shortage of howitzers was a major problem, although the supply of them was much more satisfactory by the battle's end.

September 1916 – The vital importance of artillery in the war can be gauged from this remarkable photograph of empty shell cases, piled high in this dump near Fricourt.

September 1916 – Behind the lines there were Casualty Clearing Stations. These three soldiers are recent arrivals at one near Dernancourt. Note the labels attached to their breast pockets, which are primitive medical cards indicating the nature of the wounds and the treatment given to that point.

14 September 1916 – An Advanced Dressing Station near Ginchy. With shells bursting in the background, this photograph illustrates how crucial it was to have medical services as close as possible to the action. The photograph is full of details of equipment and vehicles.

At the opening of the third phase of the British part of the Somme, on 15 September, tanks were used for the first time. The one pictured, in Chimpanzee Valley, is C19, Clan Leslie.

15 September 1916 – Here a Mark I tank is surrounded by infantry from 122nd Brigade whom it led into the eastern part of Flers, for many men this would be their first experience of a tank in battle. Of the forty-nine tanks available on 15 September, less than half actually made it to the start line. These tanks were extremely slow and mechanically unreliable; their use in small numbers has been much criticized. However, experience of battle conditions helped substantially with modifications, making the tank a more reliable and significant weapon.

15 September 1916 – A Mark I male tank – equipped with light calibre guns, whilst the female had machine-guns only. Tanks 'ditched' as much because of mechanical failure as enemy fire. The wrecks became useful landmarks in a largely featureless battlefield landscape.

15 September 1916 – Another photograph of C (for C Company) 19, Clan Leslie. The large rear wheels (rapidly abandoned in later Marks) assisted steering and the structure on top was to protect it against grenades. C19 (not the original) may be seen at the Tank Museum at Bovington.

September 1916 – Men of the 8th Seaforth Highlanders bringing defence stores up to the newly established line beyond the village of Martinpuich, captured on 15 September by the 15th (Scottish) Division. The weather broke soon afterwards, turning the Somme ground into a glutinous mixture of mud and chalk, creating exhausting and morale sapping conditions for both sides.

September 1916 – On the road to Aveluy and the front, artillery head forward and infantry are transported towards the rear. Traffic control and maintaining inadequate roads were essential tasks.

September 1916 – Aveluy Wood. This photograph of a soldier physically – or perhaps emotionally – exhausted, tells the tale of the impact of the Somme on those who fought in it.

Although a picture from the Battle of Arras, fought in the spring of 1917, it illustrates the somewhat rudimentary system of burials. However, through the work of the Imperial (now Commonwealth) War Graves Commission, this site has been transformed. Windmill Cemetery is on the Cambrai road, near Monchy le Preux.

September 1916 – When soldiers went into battle they usually left their big packs behind in the transport line. If they became casualties – in the case of wounds this meant serious enough to be moved well down the line – kit would be reallocated. In the case of those killed or confirmed prisoners, personal possessions, at least in theory, were sent to their next of kin.

September 1916 – Men of the 8th Black Watch (15th Scottish Division) on a route march (or possibly moving up to the front line area) in the tranquil conditions of a rear area in the Somme. Notice the signs of the harvest in the neatly piled stacks in the fields.

A scene of contrasts: on the left motorised transport, on the right horses pull carts with kit and casualties. Some two million men were sent back to the UK – battlefield casualties and those with illnesses such as pneumonia that could be better treated there.

15 September 1916 – Men from the 2nd Otago Regiment (2nd New Zealand Brigade) consolidating captured German trenches near Flers. The 'old' dominions provided a substantial number of troops on the Somme: the Australians three divisions, the Canadians four and New Zealand one.

New Zealand troops move across captured German trenches. Notice that many of these men are equipped with the tools to consolidate the new line.

September 1916 – Like any good soldier should, a soldier takes advantage of a quiet period to catch up on his sleep. Soldiers generally spent only a third of their time – if that – in the front line zone, although when major operations were in progress this might be rather more. Although trench life was 'routine', the threat of danger was ever present, no matter how 'quiet' the sector might be.

An officer observes the fall of shells of an artillery shoot on German trenches in the area of Leuze (known as 'Lousy' to the troops) Wood, in the southern part of British Somme operations.

September 1916 – A group of artillery observers at work on the Somme. By the autumn of 1916 what had been a generally inexperienced and under equipped gunner arm was rapidly becoming more proficient. The art of gunnery underwent considerable innovation during the war.

This photograph was taken from the Albert–Bapaume road over the original German front line system on 1 July, its course towards the village of Ovillers clearly indicated by the chalk spoil. Notice the zig-zag system, the dugouts and the bay in which the two soldiers are sitting.

After the fighting at Flers–Courcelette, the offensive continued with both major British and French attacks. Movements into the fighting trenches could not take place in daylight; only some distance in the rear could one walk around relatively freely, as these men are doing. Reliefs at night were difficult and exhausting, with the danger from German fire compounded by the truly appalling condition of the ground.

Men of the 12th Gloucesters (Bristol's Own), part of the 5th Division, move across the battlefield near Morval.

The fate of all soldiers at the front was to work as human mules. A working party moves forward to consolidate the line. It was not only a matter of the weight and the awkwardness of what they are carrying, but the treacherous ground conditions added to the ordeal.

25 September 1916 – Waves of supporting troops follow the first line of attack during the Battle of Morval.

Showers or baths were a rare luxury. However, the army did as best it could in the difficult circumstances. Such occasions were usually accompanied by the issue of clean laundry – but clean did not necessarily mean louse free.

October 1916 – Men from the 1st Wiltshires relax behind the line at Bouzincourt. The village is situated several kilometres north west of Albert. These men would soon be in action again on the Somme, involved in the fighting around Stuff Redoubt, east of Thiepval.

The war effort depended to a great extent on muscle power, human and animal. There was a massive demand for horses and mules; inevitably they were killed or died in their thousands.

October 1916 – These two photographs, of efforts to get a 60-pounder gun into position on the Bazentin ridge to add its firepower to the October fighting around Transloy, clearly show the difficulties of moving heavy artillery across battle-ravaged ground.

A gun towing tractor provides a distraction for a road mending party, standing to one side on a German road side cemetery somewhere on the Somme.

October 1916 – Men of 5th Northumberland Fusiliers queue for a haircut in Toutencourt, a village safely behind the lines to the west of Albert. Two of the men are wearing German caps.

November 1916 – Foul weather almost halted the offensive before the Battle of Ancre could commence, on 13 November. The bedraggled, soaked state of this working party near St Pierre Divion illustrates the conditions admirably.

November 1916 – British troops near Beaumont-Hamel. The village was captured by 51st (Highland Division) on 13 November, leaving Serre as the only Somme front line village still held by the Germans. The capture of Beaumont was assisted by the firing of another mine under the Hawthorn Redoubt, in the same location as that of 1 July.

November 1916 – The poor conditions were not restricted to low lying areas near rivers, like St Pierre Divion. The combination of chalk and mud stuck to everything; add lots of water and the effect was a heavy sludge. Roads in places effectively disappeared. The area had become one of man made desolation.

November 1916 – British and French troops take advantage of a mobile canteen, which clearly shows evidence of its previous existence in civilian life.

A photograph taken towards the very end of the battle, showing men from Britain, France and Germany. The Somme was the bloodiest battle of the Great War, resulting in over a million casualties.

11 November 1916 – Men of the Worcestershire Regiment take a rest behind the front. Britain's soldiers had become wiser in the ways of modern war by the end of 1916, but they were lessons learnt at enormous cost and at the expense of the lives of many of Kitchener's volunteer New Army.

By the formal end of the Somme, on 18 November 1916, the landscape of the battlefield was left utterly ruined. Nowhere did the allies advance more than six miles at a cost of some 600,000 casualties. However, subsequent actions through the winter, along with the unsatisfactory defensive line, led the Germans to withdraw eastwards up to thirty kilometres. In warfare, territorial gain is not everything.

The 51st (Highland) Division count their prisoners of war taken during their attack on Beaumont-Hamel. Each division had a prisoner of war cage and a processing system for captured men.

November 1916 – Looking over the area around Beaumont-Hamel. In the spring the war moved some miles to the east. However, with the German offensive of spring 1918, both sides here would reoccupy the trenches they held on 1 July 1916.

The village of Beaumont-Hamel after its capture during the Battle of the Somme. Beaumont – or Beaumont-Hamel – had ceased to exist by the battle's end, its location only marked by the small pile of bricks that had been the church.

December 1916 – In a trench a British soldier tests a bell that acts as a gas alarm. In January and February the British continued to mount significant operations along the Somme front, which now included much of that previously held by the French. In late February and March 1917, the Germans withdrew to the Hindenburg Line.